DAILY MEDITATIONS FOR WOMEN

INSPIRING PRACTICES FOR MANAGING EACH
DAY WITH CONFIDENCE AND CALM

ALYSSA REYNOLDS

New Autumn Press

ISBN 978-1-967413-02-7 (eBook)

ISBN 978-1-967413-03-4 (Paperback)

Published by New Autumn Press.

DISCLAIMER

This book is for informational purposes only and should not be construed as medical advice or instruction. The information in this book should never be used to diagnose, treat, prevent, or cure any disease or condition.

The author and publisher make no guarantee that this book will function in any particular way for you. Individual results may vary and are based on many factors, including but not limited to starting point, level of commitment, or genetic profile.

The author and publisher do not assume liability for accidents, injuries, delays, loss, damage, or any other consequence resulting directly or indirectly from any action or inaction you take based on the information in this book. The author and publisher are not responsible for any errors or omissions in any content herein.

CONTENTS

INTRODUCTION

Welcome to daily meditations for women! This book will help you build the positive habit of daily meditation, so you can live each day with calm and ease.

Meditation is one of the simplest ways to reduce stress and increase your quality of life. However, in order to tap into its incredible benefits, you have to establish an effective daily practice —that's where this book comes in!

By practicing one specific meditation each day for 30 days, you will unlock the powerful science-based benefits of meditation, including:

- Overcoming stress and anxiety
- Supporting emotional health
- Increasing focus and mental clarity
- Generating feelings of kindness and gratitude
- Gaining confidence and improving self-esteem
- Managing aches and pains

- Experiencing deeper sleep and increased energy

Throughout this book, you will find 30 themed and unique meditation practices—one for each day of the month. Each practice has an intention, such as cultivating positive energy or fostering courage. These meditations are specifically geared toward women, although truly anyone can benefit from this daily practice.

As women (and humans), we often experience the crushing weight of responsibility and overwhelm, which can lead to feelings of inadequacy and a lack of agency. The practices in this book are designed to combat this difficulty by offering practical tools for effectively managing life's daily challenges. As you grow in your practice, you will feel confident in your ability to handle anything life throws at you, resulting in a feeling of true empowerment.

The practices themselves are designed to be somewhat free-form. Each practice has a theme, intention, and guidance. Once you start your meditation, it's up to you to lead your practice in the way that works best for you. This allows you to explore the meditation's theme in your own way, while still having guidelines for your practice.

This format will help you to become self-sufficient in your practice, so that meditation can become a mind-body skill that you're able to access any time you need it. Each meditation has a similar structure (e.g., each meditation starts and ends with awareness of the breath), so you can easily guide yourself through the practice.

At the end of the 30 days, you'll have practiced many different meditation techniques, including mindfulness, visualization, loving-kindness, body scans, mantras, and more. As you progress through your daily meditations, you'll build on these practices and gain the ability to use them more effectively.

Soon enough, you'll be well on your way to building an intentional and diverse meditation practice that will help you overcome stress, harness inner strength, and regain your confidence.

HOW THIS BOOK WORKS

This book contains 30 varied and targeted practices that will help you tap into the many benefits of meditation. You will gain exposure to a wide variety of meditation techniques and themes, so you can choose what works best for you and build a long-term sustainable practice from there.

The variety of practices in this book ensures that you'll always have a life raft to reach for any time you need it. Whether you're in need of courage, patience, or just a good night's sleep, there is a meditation in this book that can help you!

Each practice starts with an intention and description followed by detailed guidance. To receive the full benefit from this practice, set an intention to complete one meditation every day for 30 days.

Each day, you'll find one guided meditation practice. Simply read through the practice once or twice. Familiarize yourself with the practice itself, as well as the intention and techniques.

When you're ready to begin, set an alarm for 10 minutes and guide yourself through the practice. Be sure to set an alarm with a gentle end sound like wind chimes or a gong, so you're not jarred from your practice when it goes off. You can always meditate a little past your alarm, if you're not ready to end your practice. The alarm is simply a guideline.

While I generally recommend a 10-minute alarm, so you can easily squeeze the practices into your day, feel free to set a 20-minute or longer alarm or no alarm at all. It's up to you and what works best for you on that particular day.

Always keep in mind that the guidance in this book is just that— GUIDANCE. It's not a set of rules and you don't have to follow the practices perfectly to experience positive benefits. In fact, the more you can adapt the practices to your own personal circumstances, the more powerful they will be for you.

If you're a perfectionist (like I am), consider this your opportunity to practice letting go and letting be. Your practice doesn't have to be perfect or match the guidance exactly. You should feel free to make it your own and follow each practice in the way that works best for you on that day. The goal here is consistency, not perfection.

If you'd like to delve more deeply into your daily practice, you can reflect on your experiences through journaling. This is totally optional, but can help you connect more deeply with the themes and intentions of each practice.

In your journal, you can write about thoughts and feelings that came up before, during, or after your daily practice. You can also reflect on the theme and intention of the meditation, as well as any other observations you had. This journal should NOT be a place for you to judge or evaluate your "progress" with meditation. It is simply a safe space for reflection and contemplation.

If you would like a printable PDF meditation journal with prompts to accompany your practice, you'll receive instructions on how to access it at the end of the book.

The daily meditations in this book are designed for you to experiment with different techniques and try out a multitude of practices. Once you've completed all 30 meditations (one meditation a day for 30 days), you can choose the meditations that work best for you and continue to follow them daily. You can also repeat the 30 days whenever you'd like to fortify your practice.

If you're brand new to meditation, you can start with the meditation guide in the next section. If you've practiced before and feel well-versed in what meditation is and how to get started, feel free to either skim this section or skip to Day 1.

Ready to get started?

MEDITATION GUIDE

This short introduction to meditation provides all the details you'll need to start and progress your meditation practice. This a great place to start, if you're a beginner!

What Is Meditation?

Meditation is a practice that involves focusing the mind on a particular object, thought, or activity to train attention and achieve an emotionally calm state. While our minds often wander to the past or future, meditation brings us back to the now. By being in the present moment and accepting what is, we learn to relax and let go.

When you meditate, you're not trying to turn off your thoughts or feelings. You're simply learning to observe them without judgment. We often let our thoughts and emotions take over, but with meditation, we just watch them float by. It helps us understand that our thoughts, emotions, and sensations are constantly changing.

Meditation is a skill that grows with practice. It's like a workout for your brain! Just like you would exercise a muscle if you wanted it to get stronger—meditation makes your mind more resilient so you can better cope with day-to-day stress.

When you meditate, one of the first things you'll notice is that the mind has a tendency to wander. This is completely normal and nothing to get frustrated about. The goal of meditation is not to "stop thoughts" or "clear the mind." It's to bring our minds back to the present moment when they do wander.

Meditation often involves focusing attention on one object or "anchor." A common anchor for new meditators is the breath. Observing the breath is naturally calming and easy to do. Other anchors can include sounds, thoughts, emotions, mantras, or the body. We will explore these various anchors throughout the next 30 days.

There are many positions in which you can practice meditation. Many people prefer to sit up with their eyes closed, but you can also practice lying down, standing up, or even walking. Do what works best for you.

There are both guided meditations and silent (unguided) meditations. Guided meditation can be either a written script or an audio recording that guides you through the meditation. Silent meditation is when you meditate on your own with no guidance, music, or noise. One is not better than the other—it just depends on your personal preferences and goals.

Finally, there are many different kinds of meditation. Some popular types include mindfulness meditation, loving-kindness meditation, and visualization meditation.

This book delves primarily into mindfulness meditation, although we will experiment with other kinds of meditation as well. Mindfulness meditation involves remaining in the present moment without judgment.

How to Meditate

To start, you can try this short mindfulness meditation practice. This will allow you to become comfortable with the basics before diving into the daily meditation practices.

1. Set a timer for 5 minutes.

It's best for beginners to set a timer, so you can concentrate instead of thinking about when you should end your session. It also gives you a benchmark for progressing the length of your practice.

2. Sit or lie in a quiet place where you won't be disturbed.

You can sit in a chair or on a cushion on the floor. If you're sitting on the floor, make sure your hips are higher than your knees. Place your hands on your knees either facing up (keeps your mind open and receptive) or down (keeps you grounded). You can also lie down if sitting is not comfortable for you. Meditation should never be painful, so experiment and find a position that works best for you.

3. Close your eyes and breathe naturally.

Gently close your eyes and begin to focus your attention inward. If you'd rather open your eyes, that's fine too. Just make sure you're focusing your attention inward and not looking around. One way to do this is to pick one spot in front of you to focus on and dull your gaze. Resist any urge to control the breath—just let it flow.

4. **Focus on the breath.**

Begin to focus your attention on the breath. Feel how your body moves with each inhalation and exhalation. Notice your breath moving in and out at your nose, chest, shoulders, or belly. Pay attention to the breath without controlling the pace or forcing it in any way. If your mind wanders, gently bring your attention back to the breath. For the rest of the practice, continue focusing on the sensations of breathing, bringing your mind back every time it wanders.

5. **When the timer rings, slowly bring your attention back into the room to end your practice.**

When your timer rings, don't just jump back into activity. Give your body and brain a minute of transition time. Begin to notice your surroundings: the temperature of the room, the various sounds nearby, and so on. Wiggle your fingers and toes. You can even take some time to stretch. Then, slowly open your eyes to end your practice.

Helpful Tips

As you build your daily meditation practice over the next 30 days, keep these tips in mind:

- It's not a "bad thing" for the mind to wander during meditation. Simply notice the mind wandering and bring it back to your practice as many times as you need to.

Meditation is meant to be nonjudgmental, so resist the urge to be too hard on yourself, especially at the beginning.

- It's not always necessary to sit up during meditation. Simply find a comfortable position that works best for you on that day. The meditations in this book can be practiced sitting, lying down, or even standing.

- In general, it's best to avoid falling asleep during meditation since the goal is to increase awareness (unless you're doing a sleep meditation and your intention is to fall asleep!). If you find yourself drifting off during meditation, you can keep your eyes open during your practice or change positions.

- Meditation is designed to help you cope with everyday emotions and stress. It should never feel too overwhelming or difficult to manage. If any trauma comes up during meditation and it feels like too much for you to handle, stop doing the practice and focus your attention back on your breath. Take a few deep breaths to end the meditation. Some traumas or emotional events can be too much for us to handle on our own. If you find this to be the case, please reach out to a health professional who can provide support.

- Building a consistent meditation practice is more important than the amount of time spent in each session. Just 10 minutes of daily meditation can provide transformative benefits, if you're consistent with it.

Now that you have the basics down, the best way to learn meditation is by doing! By practicing daily meditation for the next 30 days, you'll be a meditation pro in no time.

1

MEDITATION FOR TRANQUILITY

Intention: Tune into the breath to relax the body and mind.
Practices: Mindfulness, breath awareness, visualization.

*Welcome to **Day 1**! Throughout the next 30 days, you'll notice that the breath is often used as an "anchor." Your anchor is simply what you choose to focus your attention on during the meditation.*

The breath is an easy place to start because it's always with you. You simply have to pay attention to notice it. This meditation pairs practicing awareness of the breath with a soothing ocean visualization for optimal calm.

Begin this meditation in a quiet place where you won't be disturbed. Find a comfortable position either sitting up or lying down, where you feel alert yet relaxed.

You can gently close your eyes if that's comfortable. If you'd prefer to keep them open, you can rest your eyes on an object in front of you and soften your gaze.

Start to feel into your body. Notice any places of tension and just allow them to relax completely. Feel your body as it rests down into gravity, letting it be supported by the floor beneath you.

Take several full, deep breaths—in through the nose and out through the mouth. Breathe in, filling your lungs with fresh clean air, and breathe out, letting it all go. Focus on breathing in calm and relaxation and breathing out any anxiety or stress.

Next, gently let go of any control of the breath. Feel the calming wavelike movement of the breath as you breathe in and out naturally.

Begin to focus your attention on where you feel the breath most strongly. It could be at the tip of your nose or maybe at your chest or belly. Wherever you feel the breath the most—just bring your attention to rest there.

Notice how your body naturally breathes in and out. Continue to gently rest your attention on the breath as it moves in and out like the soothing waves of the ocean.

From time to time, you may find that your mind has wandered away from the breath into thinking. Don't worry—this is completely natural and expected. The mind is used to thinking and it can be difficult for it to stay still. If you notice that the mind has wandered, simply acknowledge it and gently guide your attention back to the breath.

Gradually let go of your focus on the breath and imagine yourself on a beautiful beach. Picture the warm white sand, the crystal blue water, and the soothing sounds of the waves.

Picture yourself walking slowly along the beach toward the water. You can feel the warmth of the sun on your body and the gentle ocean breeze on your face. Notice the sand getting damper as you walk, sinking into it just a little bit more.

You stop and watch the waves as they peacefully rise and fall right in front of you. As you tune into your breath again, you notice that the breath has a natural rhythm to it just like the ocean. It rises and falls in a gentle and soothing flow that makes you feel deeply relaxed.

Remember that you can always tune into this soothing breath any time you need to throughout the day. It's always there to calm and center you.

Finish the meditation by taking one more deep relaxing breath. In through the nose and out through the mouth. You are feeling happy, confident, and very relaxed.

When you're ready, you can slowly bring your attention back into the room and gently open your eyes to end this meditation.

2

BODY SCAN MEDITATION

Intention: Relax your mind by bringing awareness to the
sensations in your body.
Practices: Mindfulness, body scan, visualization.

*Welcome to **Day 2**! Most of the time, our attention is on the activity in
our minds. We're focused on our thoughts and emotions. By intention-
ally bringing focus to the body, we let go of the mental chatter and make
room for calm.*

*Body scans are typically practiced while lying on your back, but if that's
not comfortable for you, you can do this meditation sitting up or even
standing. You can lie on the floor or in your bed with a pillow under
your head and a light blanket.*

Begin this meditation in a quiet place where you won't be
disturbed. Find a comfortable position lying down on your back.

Gently close your eyes and begin to feel into your body. Feel the
weight of your body as it rests down into gravity. Allow all your
muscles to release tension as you sink deeper into the earth. Give
yourself permission to relax completely.

Allow your thoughts to calm and settle as you bring your attention to the breath. Take a slow deep breath in through the nose and out through the mouth. Feel the breath as it flows through your whole body making you feel very relaxed.

Gently move your attention down into your feet. Bring your full awareness to your feet, feeling any sensations that arise there. Notice any warmth, tingling, or pulsing. Allow any sensations you feel to just be there without judging them.

Begin to move your attention up the body into your legs. Become aware of the ankles, the calves and shins, the knees, and the thighs. Notice the places where your legs make contact with the furniture and allow them to sink more deeply into the earth as you relax completely.

Shift your awareness up into your pelvis. Become aware of the hips on either side and the buttocks in the back. Allow the pelvic area to soften as you relax more deeply.

Slowly move your awareness up into your belly. Notice the warmth in your belly and feel the soothing breath as it flows in and out like the gentle waves of the ocean.

Move your attention up into your chest. Feel the gentle rise and fall of your chest as you breathe. Notice how the breath moves in and out of the body all on its own. There is no need to control. It's safe to let go even more now.

Bring your attention into your back. Slowly move your awareness up through the back, noticing any sensations there. Allow your back to be massaged by the soothing breath as it continues to flow in and out.

Move your attention up to your shoulders. Allow your shoulders to drop back toward the ground as they relax completely. Let your attention flow down through your arms and into your hands. Feel the warmth beneath your palms and notice the sensations in each finger as you allow your hands to relax completely.

Move your attention back up the arms into your neck. If you notice any tightness or tension, allow the gentle breath to massage and loosen those areas. Notice how the body begins to soften naturally in the warm light of awareness.

Move your attention up into your face. Notice the softness in your face and allow your face to relax completely as you let go just a little bit more.

Bring your awareness to your whole head. Notice the sides of the head, the back of the head, and the top of the head. Allow your head to rest fully into gravity as you relax even more deeply.

Now imagine yourself in a beautiful place. It can be a place you know or a place from your imagination. It can be a garden, the beach, the mountains, or anywhere else you feel completely safe and relaxed.

With each exhalation, the image of this beautiful place becomes more and more vivid. As the image becomes more vivid, you find yourself relaxing more and more. You are feeling calm, happy, and deeply, deeply relaxed.

When you're ready, you can slowly bring your attention back into the room and gently open your eyes to end this meditation.

3

MEDITATION FOR ANXIETY AND STRESS RELIEF

Intention: Let go of stress and anxiety through a powerful combination of observing thoughts and calming visualization.
Practices: Mindfulness, breath awareness, awareness of thoughts, visualization.

*Welcome to **Day 3**! Observing thoughts is a simple, but very effective technique to diminish overthinking. It involves allowing thoughts to pass through your awareness without getting lost in their story. The key is simply to observe your thoughts without judgment.*

Thoughts are just mental events that we attach meaning to. When we let that meaning go, they simply become another object of our awareness. After completing this meditation, you will feel a sense of safety and deep calm.

Begin this meditation in a quiet place where you won't be disturbed. Find a comfortable position either sitting up or lying down. You can gently close your eyes or leave them open and soften your gaze.

Start by giving yourself permission to relax and let go completely. You have nothing to do right now and no place to go. Allow yourself to just settle peacefully into the here and now.

Begin tuning into the natural cycle of the breath. Place your hand on your stomach and feel into the natural rise and fall of the belly as you breathe in and out.

Notice if you're holding tension anywhere in your body and gently breathe a sense of peaceful relaxation into those areas. With each exhalation, you feel more at ease as your body relaxes more fully.

As you sit, thoughts about the past or future may arise. As these thoughts come up, remind yourself these are not what's happening right now and give yourself permission to let them go as you continue to return your attention to the calming rhythm of your breath.

As you continue to breathe deeply, you are aware of the temporary nature of thinking. You understand that the thoughts that come up in the mind are not who you are. Thoughts come and thoughts go, but who you are deep inside always remains.

Simply give yourself a little bit of space from your thoughts. Calmly observe them as they pass through your awareness without pushing them away or grabbing on to them.

Next, imagine yourself on a beautiful beach at sunset. You hear the waves gently crashing on the shore. You see a beautiful sky lit up in pink, purple, and orange. You feel the soft, warm sand underneath your feet.

The scene is so peaceful and soothing that you automatically relax. You know that on this beach, you are completely safe and can live freely. This is your safe harbor that you can visit any time you need to.

You look out and see a person walking toward you on the shore-line. This person has a warm and friendly glow about them that instantly makes you feel safe and calm.

As the person approaches, you see that it is your future self. It is the calmest and happiest version of you. Your future self tells you there is no need to worry. You're going to be okay. It's safe to let go of regrets from the past and worries about the future and just be.

You are safe. You are calm. You are free. Remind yourself of this any time you feel worried or stressed throughout the day.

Remember that any stressful or anxious thoughts that come up are just temporary. You are stronger and more powerful than these thoughts. You can let them go.

Take one more deep, slow breath. When you're ready, you can slowly bring your attention back into the room and gently open your eyes to end this meditation.

4

MEDITATION FOR FOCUS

Intention: To increase focus, feel more energized, and approach the day with productivity.
Practices: Mindfulness, breath awareness, visualization, mantra.

*Welcome to **Day 4**! This meditation pairs a powerful visualization with an effective mantra for increased focus.*

A mantra is simply a word or phrase that you repeat in your mind. By repeating the mantra, you are reinforcing the positive idea behind it. When repeated often enough, it becomes an automatic cue for the brain to engage in this positive behavior (in this case, focus).

Mantras will be used several times throughout the next 30 days for a variety of purposes. I recommend that you write down the ones that work best for you and repeat them throughout the day.

The mantra for this meditation is "Breathe in. Breathe out. Focus."

Note: Plan to do tomorrow's meditation (Day 5) at bedtime.

Begin this meditation in a quiet place where you won't be disturbed. Find a comfortable position either sitting up or lying down. You can gently close your eyes or leave them open and soften your gaze.

Start by focusing on the breath. Notice where you feel the breath most strongly. It could be at the tip of your nose or maybe in your chest or belly. Wherever you feel the breath most strongly, bring all of your focus and attention to rest there.

Continue to focus your attention on how your body naturally breathes in and out. If it helps you to focus, you can think "in" when you're breathing in and "out" when you're breathing out.

Notice how sometimes you may lose your focus as your attention starts to wander away from the breath. This is perfectly fine. By simply noticing when the mind has wandered, you have the power to bring it back and strengthen your focus once more.

Breathe in. Breathe out. Focus. Breathe in. Breathe out. Focus.

Next, imagine a small bright light. Focus all your attention on this light and concentrate on making it bigger.

The more you focus on this light, the bigger and brighter it gets. This light is your energy, your creativity, and your motivation. Observe as your focus and concentration make all those qualities grow within you.

As your concentration makes the light bigger, you can feel the warm glow of positivity and success throughout your whole body. You bask in this empowering feeling as the light continues to grow.

With every breath, the light glows brighter and bigger. Focus on the glowing light with each inhalation and exhalation.

If your mind wanders away from the light, simply bring your attention back to it. The light may dim for a moment when you shift your focus away, but you can always bring it back. Each time you bring your focus back to the light, it grows even brighter.

Breathe in. Breathe out. Focus. Breathe in. Breathe out. Focus.

This is your mantra for the day. Whenever your mind wanders during a task, just connect with the breath for a moment and think "Breathe in. Breathe out. Focus. Breathe in. Breathe out. Focus." Then, simply bring your full attention back to the task and continue growing that light of concentration and productivity. As this light continues to grow, so does your success.

You are strong. You are powerful. You can do anything you set your mind to. Just remember: Breathe in. Breathe out. Focus. Breathe in. Breathe out. Focus.

Take one more big deep breath. Breathe in feeling clear and energized. Breathe out feeling positive and motivated.

When you're ready, you can slowly bring your attention back into the room and gently open your eyes to end this meditation.

5

MEDITATION FOR PEACEFUL SLEEP

Intention: Breathe calm and total relaxation into each area of the
body.
Practices: Mindfulness, breath awareness, body scan,
visualization.

*Welcome to **Day 5**! This is a profoundly relaxing body scan meditation
that will help you unwind and sleep more deeply. The purpose of this
meditation is to calm the mind before bed and promote healing during
sleep.*

*Plan to do this meditation immediately before bed for the best results.
You should already be lying down comfortably with the lights off and
the room prepared for sleep. Allow yourself to let go and drift off. Sweet
dreams!*

Begin this meditation by lying down on your back in a comfortable position that promotes sleep. Gently close your eyes and
allow yourself to relax into bed.

Begin to tune into the natural cycle of the breath. Feel the
soothing waves of the breath as it flows in and out of the body.

Allow yourself to relax fully into the breath as you let go of all thoughts of the past or the future.

Gently move your attention into your feet. Become aware of the feet. Become aware of your heels as they rest on the bed, the bottoms of the feet, and the tops of the feet. See if you can notice the sensations in each one of your toes. Breathe calm and total relaxation into the feet as you allow them to sink more deeply into the bed.

Become aware of your legs. Notice the ankles, the calves and shins, the knees, and the thighs. Sense into the places of contact between your legs and the bed. Feel the smooth sheets beneath you and the comfortable blankets covering you. Breathe calm and total relaxation into the legs as you allow them to sink more deeply into the bed.

Bring your awareness to your pelvis. Feel the hips on either side and the buttocks in the back. Notice the gentle flow of the breath as it moves through the pelvis, down into the legs, and out through the feet. Breathe calm and total relaxation into the pelvis as you allow it to sink more deeply into the bed.

Move your attention into your stomach and chest. Become aware of the soothing rise and fall of the breath. Notice the sensations of the breath in the back of the body, as well as the front. Breathe calm and total relaxation into the stomach and chest as you allow them to sink more deeply into the bed.

Shift your attention to your shoulders, arms, and hands. Feel your arms relax down against the bed. Feel the weight of your arms at your shoulders, the weight of your forearms at your elbows, the weight of your hands at your wrists, and the weight of your fingers on your hands. Breathe calm and total relaxation all the way down into your fingers as you allow them to sink more deeply into the bed.

Bring your attention to your neck and head. Feel the soft pillow underneath your head. Relax your jaw and allow your face to soften. Breathe calm and total relaxation all the way down into your neck and head as you allow them to sink more deeply into the bed.

Next, imagine that you're resting on a cloud. The cloud is soft, fluffy, and very comfortable. On your cloud, you know that it's completely safe for you to relax and go to sleep now. Everything is going to be okay.

You are safe. You are comfortable. You are relaxed. You will experience deep sleep and sweet dreams.

Allow yourself to relax more and more deeply onto your cloud as you drift into a calm and peaceful sleep.

6

MEDITATION FOR HEALING

<u>Intention:</u> Allow the body and mind to rest, so they can heal at a
very deep level.
<u>Practices:</u> Breath awareness, visualization, mantra.

*Welcome to **Day 6**! Rest is an important part of the day because it's
when the body relaxes and recharges.*

*The mantra for this meditation is "I am safe. I am healing. I am
healthy."*

*Remember that a mantra is simply a phrase you repeat in your mind to
reinforce a positive thought pattern. Repeat this mantra throughout the
day to remind yourself of your natural healing ability.*

*Note: Tomorrow's meditation (Day 7) is best done first thing in the
morning.*

Begin this meditation in a quiet place where you won't be
disturbed. Find a comfortable position either sitting up or lying
down. You can gently close your eyes or leave them open and
soften your gaze.

Gently bring your attention to rest on the breath. Feel the healing breath as it flows through your body. As you breathe in, imagine healing and light energy filling your entire body. As you breathe out, imagine any energy that's old or stale leaving your body completely. Fill your whole body with beautiful healing light that makes you feel healthy and very relaxed.

Imagine yourself entering a beautiful garden—a secret garden known only to you. As you open the garden gate and step into it, you immediately feel a sense of healing and tranquility all around you.

You sense that this garden has powerful healing properties. It has the ability to restore your mind and body to optimal health. While you are inside the garden gate, you will heal and become stronger with each inhale and exhale.

You observe a pathway that takes you deeper into the healing power of your garden. As you walk along the path, notice what you see. Is your garden filled with flowers and trees? Are there colorful wildflowers or delicate pink roses? Perhaps there are fragrant fruit trees or a green meadow.

Whatever you see in your healing garden today is just right for you. Every flower, tree, and plant has the power to restore and revitalize you. Notice the colors, sizes, and shapes of everything around you, as you allow yourself to relax more deeply into your garden.

As the image of your garden becomes more and more vivid, you feel its healing powers grow stronger and more vibrant. You sit on a bench in the middle of your garden and bask in the comforting glow of the sun and the beautiful scent of the flowers.

You feel the warmth of the sun as it glows on your body. The light from the sun is powerful and healing. Each place that the sun touches is immediately restored and revitalized.

Feel the healing glow of the sun as the light flows through your head clearing your mind and healing your thoughts. Feel the light flow down your shoulders, arms, and into your hands. Relax more deeply into the light as it flows down your chest, stomach, back, and pelvis, healing everything in its path. Allow the healing light to flow down your legs and into your feet. Feel the healing glow of the sun from head to toe as you continue to sit in your garden allowing your body and mind to relax more deeply.

I am safe. I am healing. I am healthy.

I am safe. I am healing. I am healthy.

You stand up and begin to walk back toward the garden gate. You take in the beauty and scent of the trees and flowers as you pass through. As you prepare to leave your garden, you feel healthy and strong. You can tap into this natural healing power any time simply by thinking: I am safe. I am healing. I am healthy.

You open the garden gate and walk out into the bright and beautiful world feeling stronger and more confident than ever. You know that the healing power of the garden is always with you as you go about the rest of your day.

I am safe. I am healing. I am healthy.

I am safe. I am healing. I am healthy.

Take one more big, deep breath. When you're ready, you can slowly bring your attention back into the room and gently open your eyes to end this meditation.

7

MEDITATION FOR POSITIVE ENERGY

Intention: Increase your positive energy flow, so you can live from a place of confidence and abundance.

Practices: Breath awareness, visualization, positive memory recall.

Welcome to Day 7! This meditation will help you feel more positive and energetic throughout the day. You can do this meditation first thing in the morning or any time you need an energy boost.

It's a great practice for when you're feeling tired, listless, or uninspired. It will get you excited and ready for the day!

Begin this meditation by finding a comfortable position where you feel alert yet relaxed. If you're sitting, sit up tall and proud, lengthening up through the spine.

Take a deep breath and bring your attention inward. Notice how the breath moves in and out of your body in a gentle wavelike motion. As you breathe in, feel your body filling up with positive energy. As you breathe out, release any negativity or tiredness from your system.

Bring your attention to where you feel your center—that is, wherever you feel the most grounded in this moment. This could be at the chest or maybe the belly. Start to breathe into this space.

Visualize filling up this center with positive energy as you breathe in and out. You are fueling this power center as it grows bigger and stronger with every breath.

Imagine that you have a big, bright purple ball of light in your center. This light is filled with energy, positivity, and confidence. With each breath you take, the purple ball glows brighter and becomes more vivid.

This glowing purple ball is your inner power. It's filled with positive energy and a glowing confidence that you carry with you everywhere you go. Continue to breathe into your center as you feel the bright purple ball of light growing brighter and brighter.

Think of a memory that makes you very happy. This could be a memory from childhood or something more recent. Whichever happy memory you choose, really feel into it. Feel the glow of positivity and energy that flows through you as you picture this memory. Use that glow to make your purple ball even brighter.

As you go about your day, remember that this glowing positive energy is always inside of you. All you need to do is feel into your center and this positive light will be there to guide you.

Take one more deep breath. When you're ready, you can bring your attention back into the room to end this meditation.

8

MEDITATION FOR GRATITUDE

<u>Intention:</u> Practice gratitude for your body and appreciate the feeling of simply being alive.
<u>Practices:</u> Mindfulness, breath awareness, visualization, body scan, gratitude.

*Welcome to **Day 8**! Gratitude has been shown to improve mental and physical health, boost self-esteem, and create more loving relationships. This meditation will help you appreciate your life and body, so you can shift into a happier and more loving state.*

This practice involves sending gratitude to various parts of your body and appreciating their basic abilities, such as walking or standing. These are just suggestions and can be tailored to your individual body. For example, if you're not able to walk, simply think of something else you are grateful for. The more you can adapt this meditation to your personal life and body, the better you'll feel from it!

Start by finding a comfortable position either sitting up or lying down. Gently close your eyes and turn your attention inward.

Begin to focus your attention on the breath. Notice how your body effortlessly breathes in and out all on its own. Take a moment to appreciate the breath as it moves in and out of your body. This simple, but powerful breath gives you life and energy.

Feel a profound sense of gratitude for the breath and being alive. No matter the hardships or obstacles you've faced in life, you're still here. You're still breathing. And that alone is important to feel grateful for.

Let this powerful sense of gratitude wash over you like a glowing light. Feel the warmth and love of gratitude as it fills you up from head to toe.

Take a moment to feel into your feet. Notice the bottoms of your feet, the tops of your feet, and the toes. Say thank you to your feet for all they do for you each day—from supporting you while you stand up to giving you the gift of walking.

Feel gratitude for your legs. Notice the ankles, the calves and shins, the knees, and the thighs. Say thank you to your legs for all they do for you each day, helping you to sit, stand, and walk.

Notice your stomach. Feel the gentle rise and fall of your belly as you breathe. Say thank you to your stomach for all it does for you each day, including the very important task of digesting your food.

Feel into your chest. Notice the beat of your heart, the beat that keeps you alive and well. Say thank you to your heart for all it does for you each day—for giving you the ability to love others and feel your emotions.

Become aware of your shoulders, arms, and hands. Notice any sensations in your hands, such as warmth or tingling. Your hands do so much for you. They hold and carry things for you all day long, as well as allow for the sensation of touch. Say thank you to your hands for all they do for you each day.

Notice your neck and head. Relax your jaw and forehead—allow your face to just soften. Maybe even feel a small smile on the corners of your lips. Say thank you to your neck and head for all they do for you each day. Tap into gratitude for your brain, which gives you the ability to think, store knowledge, and access memories.

Feel the warm and loving glow of gratitude from head to toe as you say thank you to your whole body. Your body is your oldest friend and steadiest companion. It has supported you your entire life. When you were happy, sad, or scared, your body was there for you. Take a few moments to really appreciate that.

Now think about one thing you're grateful for today. It could be a person you love, a good book that you read, the home that you live in, or even something as simple as having running water or food on the table. Let the gratitude you feel for this one thing flow through your entire body like a warm glowing light, making you feel happy and safe.

Take one more deep breath. Once again, tap into deep gratitude for simply being alive. Appreciate this breath, this moment, and this precious life.

When you're ready, slowly bring your attention back into the room and open your eyes to end this meditation.

9

MEDITATION FOR COMPASSION

Intention: Send well-wishes to yourself and others.
Practices: Mindfulness, breath awareness, loving-kindness, self-reflection, compassion.

Welcome to Day 9! This meditation is based on an age-old practice called loving-kindness (also known as metta meditation).

Loving-kindness is a powerful practice that cultivates compassion by sending well-wishes to yourself and others by repeating phrases, such as: "May you be happy. May you be healthy. May you be safe. May you live with ease." It is a form of self-care that fosters kindness and well-being.

This meditation is a bit different from the previous ones and may take some practice. Just be kind and patient with yourself. Over time, you will experience stronger connections and a greater sense of peace within yourself.

Start by finding a comfortable position either sitting up or lying down. Gently close your eyes and bring your attention to your breath.

As you notice the calming breath flow in and out, reflect for a moment on how the breath is the common thread between all beings.

Bring into your awareness that all people, no matter how different we may seem, have one simple thing in common: We all breathe. We all have the ability to feel into and experience the life force of the breath. Reflect on this as you continue to rest attention on your own breath.

Start this compassion practice by offering loving-kindness to yourself. Remember that you are just as worthy of your own compassion as anybody else. This is an act of self-love and self-care.

Begin by saying silently to yourself: "May I be happy. May I be healthy. May I be safe. May I live with ease." Focus your attention on these compassionate words and the positive intention behind them, as you wish yourself well.

Bring to mind a person who has a positive influence on your life. Someone who makes you smile and fills your heart with joy. Picture this person sitting in front of you looking into your eyes.

Send the same compassionate well-wishes to them that you did for yourself: "May you be happy. May you be healthy. May you be safe. May you live with ease."

If your mind wanders away from these statements, that's perfectly okay. Just gently guide yourself back and repeat: "May you be happy. May you be healthy. May you be safe. May you live with ease."

Bring to mind someone who has a neutral presence in your life. This could be a coworker or neighbor whom you don't know very well. It could even be a cashier at the grocery store or a barista at your local café.

Although you don't know this person very well, you can still wish them well and show genuine compassion toward them. This person wants to be happy and free of suffering just like you do.

Picture this person as vividly as you can and send them the same well-wishes: "May you be happy. May you be healthy. May you be safe. May you live with ease."

Now bring to mind a difficult person in your life. Someone you have trouble getting along with or whose words or actions may have hurt you.

Although it may be difficult to send this person your compassion, doing so is actually an act of self-care. You are not excusing this person for what they did—however, by showing them even a small bit of compassion, you are healing yourself and the world around you. If someone else has hurt you, it is only because they, themselves, are suffering. By giving them your compassion, you are showing even greater compassion and love toward yourself.

Send the same well-wishes to this person: "May you be happy. May you be healthy. May you be safe. May you live with ease."

If this feels too challenging for you right now, that's perfectly okay. Just go back to sending loving-kindness to yourself. This can be a difficult practice and it takes some patience. Always show yourself love and compassion first and foremost, and do whatever is needed to take care of yourself in this moment.

Now offer your compassionate well-wishes to all beings everywhere. All people, all animals, all plants— everything in existence. "May we all be happy. May we all be healthy. May we all be safe. May we all live with ease."

Remember that the common thread between all of us is the breath. Take a deep inhale and, on your exhale, send compassion to all beings everywhere. "May we all be happy. May we all be healthy. May we all be safe. May we all live with ease."

Take one final deep breath. When you're ready, open your eyes to end this meditation.

10

MEDITATION FOR HAPPINESS

Intention: Experience a sense of joy and positivity.
Practices: Visualization, imagination, positive memory recall.

*Welcome to **Day 10**! This is a fun and light-hearted meditation that uses your imagination to foster feelings of happiness.*

Imaginative play is beneficial to both kids and adults, as it builds a sense of creativity and contentment. You will be using your imagination to create your "happy place" filled with your favorite food, childhood memories, and people.

If you can't think of a fond childhood memory during this meditation, that's totally fine. Any happy memory from adulthood will work just as well.

Begin by finding a comfortable position either sitting up or lying down. You can gently close your eyes or keep them open and soften your gaze. Take a few deep breaths, feeling relaxation and positive energy flow through you.

Bring to mind a place that makes you genuinely happy. This could be a place you know or a place in your imagination. It could be the beach, your favorite room at home, a beautiful garden, or an amusement park. It could even be the setting from your favorite book or movie. Just choose a place where you feel happy, joyful, and relaxed. This is your happy place that you can go back to any time.

Imagine that your favorite food is being served in this place—24/7. No matter what, you can always get your favorite food here. You never get tired of it and it never expands your waistline. When you eat this food, you just feel happy and filled with joy.

Think about your favorite thing from childhood. It could be a stuffed animal or maybe a game you liked to play. It could even be a friend with whom you loved spending time.

Imagine that this thing or person is in your happy place with all the wonderful feelings and memories that it's connected to. Feel that childlike wonder flow from deep inside, giving you a sense of fun and playfulness.

Imagine that all the people you love and care about are in your happy place. The people who make you smile, who take care of you, and who fill you with joy. They're all here together in your wonderful place. They're all smiling and laughing and just having fun, all together.

Think about anything else you want to add to your happy place to make it even more joyful. Maybe a bath that you can relax in or a good book you can get lost in. Just something simple that makes you smile.

As you add more things to your happy place, it never gets crowded. It simply expands to accommodate more joy, more fun, and more love.

Picture this happy, wonderful place filled with all the things and the people that you love. Imagine it all as vividly as you can, including the colors, shapes, and sizes all around you.

Remember that you can return to this happy place any time you need to get in touch with the cheerful side of life. It's always there for you in your heart.

Take one more deep breath in and just take a moment to smile—a big, real, genuine smile. Smile to yourself knowing that, although it's fun to imagine your happy place, simply being alive and feeling into this breath is enough to experience true joy and fulfillment. Let your smile fill you up with a radiant energy that you'll carry with you into the rest of your day.

When you're ready, bring your attention back into the room and gently open your eyes to end this meditation.

11

MEDITATION FOR ACCEPTANCE

Intention: Accept the inevitable ups and downs of life with a sense
of calm.
Practices: Mindfulness, breath awareness, visualization,
acceptance.

*Welcome to Day 11! As humans, we tend to resist pain and chase
pleasure. While this is normal, it is a cycle that creates suffering. Acceptance has been shown to reduce stress and promote better quality of life.*

*Stress often comes from pushing back against life and not accepting the
way things are in the moment. We believe that we should be happy all
the time, so when we're not, we think something is wrong. But in reality,
pain and pleasure are both a natural part of life and will continue to
coexist, no matter what we do. The most effective way to maintain a
sense of calm amid life's natural ups and downs is to approach them
with an attitude of acceptance.*

*Acceptance doesn't mean we give up or stop trying to improve. It simply
means that we accept that life has both happy and sad moments, and we*

allow them to be. When you truly accept where you're starting from, in this moment, that's when real positive change can take place.

Begin this meditation in a comfortable position either sitting up or lying down. Gently close your eyes and bring your attention inward.

Start to focus on your breath, observing as it rises and falls within you. There is no need to control. There is no need to change. In this moment, we are simply observing and accepting the natural ebb and flow of the breath.

Use your breath to anchor you in the present moment by bringing your attention to your exhale. Observe how the exhalation flows out of your body in a wavelike motion. With each exhalation, settle more deeply into the here and now. Allow your body and mind to just relax, soften, and let go.

Life can sometimes make us feel like we're being tossed by the waves of the ocean. It's constantly changing, bringing us a mix of happy moments, difficult moments, and everything in between.

While it's natural to want to be happy all the time, resisting difficult experiences, such as anger, sadness, or pain, only makes life more challenging. The key is to accept these experiences as they arise and allow them to pass through us, just like the fluid motion of the exhale.

Imagine that the ups and downs of life are like waves on the ocean, continuously rising and falling. If you resist the natural rise and fall of these waves, you will feel tossed about at the mercy of each one. However, if you simply observe the waves with an outlook of acceptance, you will feel much more relaxed and balanced.

Imagine that you are on a beautiful ship making its way through the sea. You can observe the rise and fall of the waves from the deck of your ship. You may even feel the waves moving up and down beneath you. However, this doesn't change your course. You are strong and steady, moving through the waves of life with acceptance and clarity.

Rest on the deck of your ship, as you allow the waves of life to move gently beneath you, accepting each one as it comes. Let the wavelike movement of the breath carry you gently from one moment to the next.

As you inhale, bring a sense of openness and acceptance to all of your experience. As you exhale, feel a sense of relaxation and balance deep inside of you.

No matter what happens in life, you can accept it and you can manage it. You can do what needs to be done to move forward with hope and clarity.

Take a few more deep breaths—riding the wave of each exhalation with calm acceptance. When you're ready, you can bring your attention back into the room and gently open your eyes to end this meditation.

12

MEDITATION FOR COURAGE

Intention: Conquer your fears, so you can move forward and take
positive action.
Practices: Breath awareness, visualization, mantra.

*Welcome to Day 12! Through this meditation, you will unlock your
unique source of inner power and learn to tap into it, whenever you
require a boost of confidence and strength. Life can be scary and difficult
at times, but courage helps us maintain a sense of calm and balance,
even during extreme challenges.*

*So often, fear holds us back from living our best life. We are inherently
afraid of change and often stay in our comfort zones because of it. The
following guided visualization will help you access the strength and
inner power that is inside all of us.*

*The mantra for this meditation is "I am strong. I am confident. I can do
this."*

Begin this meditation by finding a position where you feel confident yet relaxed and gently close your eyes. If you're sitting, sit up

tall and lengthen through your spine. Feel into your inner strength and allow energy to flow through you as you breathe.

Bring your awareness to the breath. Start to draw your breath all the way down into the belly, letting it expand, and then exhale completely, letting it all go.

True courage comes from the willingness to face our fears. As the saying goes, fear cannot exist in the light, only in the dark. Start by bringing fear out into the light of awareness.

Bring to mind an area of your life where you may be feeling insecure, doubtful, or afraid. Allow this part of your life to come to the forefront of your mind. Let the object, person, or circumstance that is causing you fear into the light of your awareness and just observe.

If this becomes too difficult for you, that's totally fine. Just bring your awareness back to the breath—taking two deep breaths, filling and emptying the belly completely. Then, gently bring your awareness back to facing your fear.

Now imagine that there is a bright fire within you that burns through all fears and obstacles. This fire is your inner power and strength. Feel into the warmth of this fire deep inside your belly, as you continue to breathe deeply.

Visualize a flame at the center of your belly—a flame of total confidence that melts away all fear and self-doubt. As you continue to breathe deeply into your belly, filling up completely, you feel the flame growing brighter and bolder with each inhale and exhale.

When we connect deeply with our center, we build an inner power and strength that can't be destroyed. It simply grows brighter and bolder with each breath, burning through all fears and obstacles. As the flame grows brighter, you grow bolder.

Allow your breath to connect you with this powerful force as you continue to breathe deeply into your center, observing as the flame grows brighter and bolder with every breath.

Bring back into mind the one area of your life where you wished for more courage and strength. Imagine the flame inside of you burning through all fears and obstacles, until you're left with pure courage.

Without your fears distracting you, you are now free to imagine the most positive outcome for this area of your life. What does it feel like to take confident and empowered action that moves you forward?

Repeat to yourself: I am strong. I am confident. I can do this.

I am strong. I am confident. I can do this.

Take one more deep breath filling the belly on the inhale and letting your fear melt away on your exhale. Remember that this powerful flame is always inside of you, helping you move forward with positivity and courage.

When you're ready, you can gently bring your attention back into the room and open your eyes to end this meditation.

13

MEDITATION FOR DEEP RELAXATION

Intention: Reach a level of consciousness between wakefulness
and sleep to experience a very deep level of relaxation.
Practices: Breath awareness, deep relaxation.

*Welcome to **Day 13**! This meditation will help you relax at very deep
levels. It's very effective for any time you need to relax your body and
mind, especially before bed or during times of high stress.*

*During this meditation, you will reach a level of consciousness between
wakefulness and sleep. This is the state that you reach right before you
fall asleep, where you are awake but deeply relaxed. You don't need to do
anything to reach this state of relaxation—just simply be.*

*Note: If you would like to listen to an audio version of this meditation
recorded with special music, you can access it at flaxseedsandfairytales.
com/relaxation. The music used in this recording contains binaural
beats and is tuned to 432 Hz to help your brain reach the deepest levels
of calm more quickly.*

Begin this meditation lying down on your back in a comfortable position. Gently close your eyes and begin to focus your attention on the relaxing breath.

Take a deep breath in and breathe out fully, letting it all go. Place one hand on your belly and feel into the gentle rise and fall of the body as you breathe.

Take a slow deep breath in, feeling the belly expand underneath your hand. Then, breathe out, feeling the belly deflate as you release completely. With each breath, you feel your body relaxing more deeply into the earth. You feel a profound sense of calm and safety deep inside.

Allow the sensation of deep relaxation to wash over you as you continue to breathe. Keep your focus on the calming wavelike motion of the belly, as you breathe in and out. Let go of all thoughts and allow yourself to drift into a state of calm that is just between wakefulness and sleep.

If your mind wanders away from the breath, gently bring it back to the movement of your belly and let peace wash over you, once again. Your breath is slow and deep as you sink more fully into the earth. Let go completely and just rest.

You are safe. You are calm. You are at peace. Everything is right in your world. There is nothing to do. Nothing to think about. Just relax and breathe.

Your mind is relaxed. Your body is relaxed. Your world is at peace. It is safe for you to let go of your thoughts and just focus on your breath. All is well.

You feel a sense of peace and tranquility deep inside of you. You realize that this profound relaxation is always inside of you. You simply need to focus on your breath and relax into your body to feel it. When thoughts enter your mind, just let them go. You don't need them in this state of deep relaxation. All you need is your breath.

You are safe. You are calm. You are at peace.

As you prepare to reemerge from this state of deep relaxation, remember that it is always there for you when you need it. All you need to do is focus on the breath deep inside your belly and you'll feel a sense of peace once more.

If you're going to sleep, you can continue to focus on the breath in the belly until you drift off. Otherwise, begin to slowly reengage with your surroundings.

When you're ready, you can begin to wiggle your fingers and your toes. Begin to notice the sounds around you and gently open your eyes to end this meditation.

14

MEDITATION FOR SELF-LOVE

<u>Intention:</u> Foster a sense of self-love and engage in self-care.
<u>Practices:</u> Visualization, loving-kindness, compassion.

*Welcome to **Day 14**! This meditation is similar to the Meditation for Compassion on Day 9, but instead of sending well-wishes to others, you will be sending them to yourself. It's particularly effective for when you need a self-esteem or confidence boost!*

Remember that building loving relationships with others, starts with loving yourself first and foremost. Self-love is <u>not</u> selfish. It's nurturing yourself, so you can take care of others. This meditation will help you do just that through a powerful visualization designed to foster self-love and self-care. When we send ourselves love, the body and mind relax and we feel a sense of peace deep within.

The loving-kindness phrases for this meditation are "May I be happy. May I be healthy. May I be safe. May I live with ease."

Begin this meditation in a comfortable position either sitting up or lying down. Choose this position with a great sense of care for your own well-being. Listen to your body with love and position it in such a way that feels right to you.

Take a deep breath in and slowly release it. Allow the gentle and loving breath to relax your whole body and mind.

Bring to mind an image of yourself as a child. It doesn't matter which age you choose—just focus on whatever feels right.

Notice how this child looks and is feeling. Just like everyone else— this child simply wants to feel loved, safe, and happy.

Keep your focus on this image of yourself as a child, young and vulnerable. Like all beings, this child thrives on love and care. She needs your love and care in order to grow and be strong.

Begin to send your love and well-wishes to your younger self. "May I be happy. May I be healthy. May I be safe. May I live with ease." Hold the image of yourself as a child in your mind as you continue to repeat these well-wishes.

As your younger self absorbs all your love and care, you begin to feel a warm glow throughout your body. This is the powerful feeling of self-love filling your heart, body, and mind.

Hold on to this warm feeling as you gently let go of the image of yourself as a child. Allow the glow of self-love to fill you up from head to toe.

Turn your attention onto yourself as you are now. You are every bit as worthy of your own love as the child you visualized earlier. Just like the child, you thrive on feelings of love and safety.

Focus on yourself as you are now and repeat the same well-wishes. You can place one hand over your heart as you recite these phrases in your mind: "May I be happy. May I be healthy. May I be safe. May I live with ease."

Bring to mind one thing you really love about yourself. This could be a physical trait, a personality trait, or a talent that you have—anything at all that you feel good about. If you can't think of anything, that's perfectly fine. You can simply love the fact that you are alive and breathing.

Bring this one thing you love about yourself into the light of awareness and feel the warm glow of self-love wash over you. Feel into how amazing and powerful you truly are, especially when you take the time to love and appreciate yourself.

You are beautiful. You are strong. You are enough.

Remember that no one is more worthy of your love than yourself. We all make mistakes. No one is perfect. But, self-love is not dependent on getting things right or being flawless. It is simply about accepting and loving yourself unconditionally, exactly as you are right now.

Take one more slow deep breath in and let it all go. When you're ready, you can gently bring your attention back into the room and open your eyes to end this meditation.

15

MEDITATION FOR BALANCE

<u>Intention:</u> Experience balance in your mind and body, so you can invite more balance into your day-to-day life.
<u>Practices:</u> Mindfulness, breath awareness, body awareness, visualization.

*Welcome to **Day 15**! This meditation will help you to feel centered and in harmony with the world around you. When you become overwhelmed with a long to-do list, this practice will help you take your day one step at a time.*

When it comes to overwhelm, remember to always start with the most important task first and work up from there. Try not to get caught up in doing everything at once—just focus on the <u>next</u> task that needs to get done and complete this task mindfully. If your mind wanders to everything else you need to do, just bring it back to the present moment and focus on completing this one important task first. Once you've finished, you can move on to completing the next task with the same approach.

Discovering this sense of balance will make your busy lifestyle feel manageable and help to prevent burnout. This is a form of self-care that promotes both health and well-being.

Similar to Day 8, this meditation asks that you observe specific parts of the body to find balance. If you find that the guidance doesn't apply to your body, then always feel free to adapt it to what works best for you!

Find a comfortable position that promotes a sense of wakefulness. If you're sitting up, you can sit on a chair or cross-legged on a cushion. Sit up tall through the spine and balance your weight evenly on both sides. However you choose to position your body —make sure that you feel a sense of balance.

Take a deep inhale and slowly exhale. Notice how the in-breath and out-breath balance each other out. For every in-breath, there is exactly one out-breath that follows. One cannot exist without the other—they function in harmony. Noticing the breath creates a natural sense of balance in the body. The breath maintains its own equilibrium as it moves in and out.

Begin to notice how the body has a natural sense of balance as well. You have two hands and two feet, as well as a right and left side of your body. Feel into that balance as you rest more deeply into your seat.

Imagine that you are walking along a beautiful river. The river is peaceful and quiet. There's nothing around you but the sounds of nature. As you walk, you notice all sorts of rocks on the bank of the river.

There are rocks of all different shapes and sizes. Some are flat and others are round. Take a moment to really visualize each rock as you continue to walk along the river.

When you get to the edge of the river, you see a small rock pile. Each rock is balanced carefully on top of another to create a stable structure. You notice that the largest rock is on the bottom. The rock on top of that one is still large, but slightly smaller. The rock on top of that one is even smaller. The sizes of the rocks get smaller as the pile rises.

The rocks are all different sizes, shapes, and colors yet they maintain a perfect balance—one on top of the other in perfect harmony. A well-balanced life is just like this rock pile. In order to find balance in life, you must always start with the largest "rock" first. This rock represents your main priority. This is your foundation and each area of life builds on top of that one.

You give the most time and energy to the larger rocks, which will allow them to support the smaller rocks. Together, they create a balanced and peaceful life.

Whenever you feel overwhelmed and stressed, just remember to start with the largest rock first, your main priority in this moment, and build up from there. Take life one moment at a time and work your way up.

Take one last look at the river and breathe in a sense of balance. As you breathe out, let this balance flow into your body, your mind, and your life.

When you're ready, you can gently bring your attention back into the room and open your eyes to end this meditation.

16

MEDITATION FOR FORGIVENESS

Intention: To practice forgiveness and letting go.
Practices: Breath awareness, visualization, emotional release,
compassion.

*Welcome to **Day 16**! This practice will help you let go and learn to forgive yourself and others.*

Many of us can be reluctant to forgive because we see it as letting others "off the hook." However, when we hold on to anger, resentment, and hate, we are only hurting ourselves. As the saying goes, "Holding on to anger is like drinking poison and expecting the other person to die." In the end, it hurts you a lot more than it does the other person.

Forgiveness doesn't mean you're excusing someone for hurting you. It simply means you are preventing yourself from experiencing further pain by letting go of anger and resentment. It's an act of self-care that will improve your mental and physical health.

If it's difficult for you to open up to the idea of forgiveness, you can think of this as the "Meditation for Letting Go of Anger." When you let go of anger, you are free. This doesn't mean you have to be friends with the person who hurt you— it simply means that you are no longer carrying their burden in your heart.

Letting go of old resentments will help you to experience more inner peace and calm. After completing this meditation, you will feel lighter and ready to move forward with positivity.

Begin this meditation in a comfortable position either sitting up or lying down. Find a position where you feel alert yet relaxed.

Take a deep breath in, filling your lungs completely, and then let it all go. Breathe in fresh clean air with each inhale, as you allow old, stale air to leave your body with each exhale.

The practice of forgiveness is an important but difficult one. It's natural to hold on to resentment or anger when someone has hurt you. However, in doing so, you're only causing yourself further pain.

Forgiveness isn't about excusing the other person—it's simply about freeing yourself from the hurtful emotions. Be sure to practice self-care and send yourself plenty of love during this practice. If it ever becomes too difficult for you, you can always return your focus to the breath and resume this practice when you're ready.

Bring to mind someone you have yet to forgive. It could be a loved one, someone from your past, or even yourself. Continue to breathe deeply as you picture this person in your mind. Think about the situation that has caused you to bear negative feelings toward this person.

Notice how you feel when you think about this person and the situation. Do you feel angry, sad, or maybe resentful? Whatever you feel, simply remember that you are in a safe space and continue to breathe through it.

The key to forgiveness is creating separation between what this person has done to hurt you and the person themselves. When someone has caused us pain, it can be difficult to see past these hurtful feelings. This makes it hard for us to forgive and release the burden of anger from inside of us.

As you focus on this person, observe the negative energy that you've associated with them. Notice the burden of this feeling in your body.

Next, imagine yourself releasing the negativity that's tied to this person. Feel it drain out of your body with every breath.

Once you pull the negative energy of the situation away, all you're left with is the person. This person simply wants to be loved and feel happy, just like you do. Whatever this person has done to hurt you, they did it because they themselves are hurting in some way.

You're not required to let this person off the hook or excuse what they've done to you. You don't necessarily have to like this person or spend time with them. You are simply letting go of the negative energy that's lingered inside of you. You are realizing that the person and the hurt they've caused you are separate. You can let the hurt go. You can forgive. You can move on.

As you feel these negative feelings leave your body, you are beginning to feel lighter. Take a deep breath in and a slow breath out, releasing all the negative energy completely. Feel the anger, the resentment, and the pain draining from your body.

Take one more deep breath, feeling the fresh clean air inside your lungs. You have forgiven. You are free.

When you're ready, you can gently bring your attention back into the room and open your eyes to end this meditation.

17

MEDITATION FOR LOVING RELATIONSHIPS

<u>Intention:</u> Create more loving relationships.
<u>Practices:</u> Visualization, compassion, connection.

*Welcome to **Day 17**! This meditation will help you build a more loving relationship with a partner, child, family member, or anyone else you feel a close personal connection to.*

You can do this meditation on your own or together with a loved one to build a stronger bond. The guidance will tell you to imagine looking into the eyes of someone you love. If you choose to do this meditation with another person, you can look directly into their eyes instead. I recommend that you sit about one to two feet apart facing each other. If looking into their eyes feels too intense, you can simply sit or lie next to them with your eyes closed or gaze softened.

Whether you do this practice on your own or with a loved one, it will help you to approach your relationships with more love and equanimity. Relationships are about connection, patience, and understanding. This meditation will help you foster these positive intentions.

Begin this meditation in a comfortable position either sitting up or lying down. Find a position that feels open and receptive. Gently close your eyes or soften your gaze. If you're doing this practice together with a loved one, you can sit facing each other and look into the other's eyes. Relax your body completely and connect to your breath.

Start by feeling into your body. If there are any areas of tension or tightness, see if you can allow them to soften. Keep your body as relaxed and open as possible.

Imagine looking into the eyes of someone you love. This could be a partner, a child, a friend, or anyone else you feel a deep and personal connection to.

Bring this person into focus. Notice what they look like and how they make you feel. Picture your loved one in a way that brings a smile to your face and makes you feel connected to them.

Imagine that this is the only moment you have with this person. What would you tell them? How would you communicate your feelings toward them?

Tap into the deep sense of connection you feel with this other person. Think about everything that makes them unique and special to you. Notice how it feels in your body to think of your loved one in this way.

Imagine yourself continuing to look into this person's eyes. Notice the compassion, wisdom, and strength in those eyes. Feel the depth of your love for them.

Visualize your heart opening with love. Allow this love to flow from your heart into your loved one's. Feel the bond and connection opening between you, as you allow the love to flow unconditionally.

While you and your loved one may have differences and experience conflict from time to time, at the core of your being, you are the same. You both want the same things—to be healthy, to be happy, to be safe, and to feel loved. In a strong and loving relationship, you allow these things to flow openly between you. This is your bond. This is your connection. Feel into this connection, as you allow these positive feelings of love and openness to flow through you.

Let this image of your loved one go and focus your attention back on the breath. Notice how your body feels with all this positive and loving energy flowing through it.

Take one more slow deep inhale and exhale it completely. Allow your breath to be saturated with love and caring for yourself and others. When you're ready, you can gently bring your attention back into the room and open your eyes to end this meditation.

18

MEDITATION TO RELEASE TENSION

Intention: Release tension from the mind and body.
Practices: Mindfulness, breath awareness, deep breathing, body scan.

*Welcome to **Day 18**! When we're feeling stressed or anxious, we tend to hold tension in the physical body as well. We instinctively tighten our muscles as a fight-or-flight response. This is because the brain and body perceive the stressful emotion as a "threat" and prepare to either fight or run away.*

When we release tension in the physical body, we are sending a message to our brain that we are safe. The fight-or-flight response gets turned off and we automatically relax.

You can do this meditation before bed or any time you need to release tension in the mind and body. It's also very effective for relieving muscle pain or headaches resulting from tension. You will feel a sense of looseness and deep relaxation, as your body lets go and the muscles unwind.

As with every practice, remember that you don't have to follow the guidance perfectly. Simply start at the top of your head and release the tension in every part of your body, in turn, while continuing to breathe deeply. Feel free to spend extra time on the parts of your body that need it the most.

Begin this meditation in a comfortable position lying down. You can rest your head on a pillow and cover yourself with a light blanket. Gently close your eyes and bring your attention to the breath.

Start by taking three deep breaths in through the nose and out through the mouth. With each breath, allow your body to become heavier as it relaxes into the earth.

Begin to focus on your exhalation. Notice how with each exhalation, the body lets go a little bit more.

Bring your attention to your head. Notice any tension in the muscles of your face and allow them to soften. Release the forehead, the muscles around the eyes, the cheeks, and the jaw. We carry a lot of tension in the jaw, so just allow it to hang open and loose.

Notice any tension in the mind. Observe any thoughts or stories that are replaying in your mind and give yourself permission to let them go. You don't need them for this practice. Your attention is focused solely on the body and the breath.

Allow your entire head to be heavy as it relaxes into the pillow beneath you. Take a deep breath in and let everything go on your exhale.

Bring your attention to your neck. Feel the muscles in the back of your neck and in your throat. Allow all the muscles in your neck to just relax. Feel the muscles in your neck begin to soften as you rest back into gravity—allowing the earth to support your body fully.

Notice your shoulders, arms, and hands. With each exhalation, allow these areas to become heavy and loose. You can open and close your hands, as you allow the tension to dissolve completely.

Bring your attention to your chest and belly. Feel the rise and fall of the chest and belly as you continue to breathe deeply. With each exhalation, let go just a little bit more as your body sinks into the surface beneath you.

Bring your attention to your back. Notice how the breath is just as present in the back of the body as it is in the front. Allow the gentle breath to massage and release all the tension in your back as you relax more deeply.

Notice your hips, pelvis, and buttocks. We carry a lot of tension in these areas, so just allow them to gently release. Let your buttocks sink into the surface beneath you, as your pelvis and hips release with each exhale.

Bring your attention to your legs. Notice the thighs, the knees, the calves, and the shins. Feel your legs growing heavier and warmer in the light of your awareness. Allow all the tension to release from these areas as you sink more deeply into the earth.

Notice your ankles and feet. Keep breathing deeply and allow any remaining tension in your body to release through your feet on the exhale. Just let everything go.

Take a full deep inhale and, as you exhale, sweep the breath from the top of your head all the way down and out through your feet. Feel each part of the body relax with the exhale as you let that last bit of tension go. Your body feels loose and relaxed as you sink even more deeply into the earth.

Take one last deep breath, filling your body with relaxation and calm. When you're ready, slowly bring your attention back into the room and gently open your eyes to end this meditation.

19

MEDITATION FOR MOTIVATION

Intention: Tap into feelings of motivation and productivity.
Practices: Breath awareness, visualization, mantra.

*Welcome to **Day 19**! In this meditation, you will be capturing the energy of a place that excites you, in order to build motivation. You'll learn to direct this inspirational energy into your daily tasks, so you can stay productive.*

This is a great practice for when you feel low energy, bored, or uninspired. You can do this meditation in the morning to build motivation for the day or any time you need an extra boost of productivity. It will help you stay positive, so you can accomplish tasks quickly and successfully.

The mantra for this meditation is "I am motivated. I am inspired. I can do it." Repeat these phrases in your mind whenever you need a motivational boost!

Begin this meditation in a comfortable position that makes you feel empowered. If you choose to sit, be sure to sit up tall through your spine. Experience positive energy flowing through you, helping you to sit up just a little bit taller.

Take a deep breath in, filling your body with energy. Then, breathe out, letting go of any boredom or lethargy. With each breath, you feel more empowered and excited for the day ahead.

Bring to mind a place that inspires you. This could be a place in nature like the beach or the mountains. It could be a city sidewalk or an amusement park. Simply choose a place that excites you!

Visualize this place as vividly as you can. Imagine the colors, shapes, and sizes of everything around you. What does it smell like? What sounds do you hear?

Feel into the energy of this inspirational place. A place that inspires has a strong positive energy associated with it. Just take a moment to vividly experience what this place feels like to you.

Imagine that the energy from this inspirational place is flowing through you. Feel the same sense of excitement you experience when visiting this place rushing through you, leaving energy and motivation in its path.

Imagine that the inspiration you feel from this place is bubbling up inside of you and that you have the power to direct this energy anywhere you choose. This inspiration is unlimited and you can use it to motivate yourself any time you need it.

Choose to direct this inspirational energy into the next task you do. No matter how small or mundane the task is—approach it with all the same enthusiasm that you have for this special place. It's all inside of you now. You can access it any time you need to.

I am motivated. I am inspired. I can do it.

I am motivated. I am inspired. I can do it.

No task is too big or too small for you succeed in. With unlimited inspirational energy at your disposal, you will feel motivated in all that you do. Whenever you feel bored or tired, simply tap into the energy from your inspirational place and you will find the motivation you need.

Take a few more deep breaths. With each in-breath, feel a surge of motivation flow through your body. With each out-breath, feel that motivation becoming stronger. Feel the rush of inspiration and enthusiasm growing within you with every breath.

I am motivated. I am inspired. I can do it.

I am motivated. I am inspired. I can do it.

When you're ready, you can start to bring your attention back into the room and open your eyes to end this meditation.

20

MEDITATION FOR PEACE

Intention: Experience a deep and unwavering sense of peace.
Practices: Mindfulness, breath awareness, visualization, emotional release, loving-kindness, compassion.

*Welcome to **Day 20**! This meditation will help you get in touch with the deep sense of peace that is inside all of us. At the core of who you are, there is always peace.*

Thoughts, emotions, and physical pain are simply passing states. They may temporarily cloud your peace, but true inner peace is as vast as the sky—the rest are simply passing clouds. When you detach from thoughts, emotions, and physical sensations, you'll find a peace and tranquility you've never felt before.

Once you connect with this inner peace, you can send it out into the world. Although the world is far from peaceful, there is always hope for tomorrow. It all starts with connecting to the compassion and love that are deep inside. The more we connect with that center, the more at peace we are.

Begin this meditation in a comfortable position either sitting up or lying down. Gently close your eyes and bring your attention to the breath at your core. Feel how the breath moves in and out at the center of the belly, creating a strong and stable foundation. Take a full deep breath in through the nose and out through the mouth, as you settle more deeply into your seat.

Deep inside each of us, there is a light that never dims. This light is inner peace. It comes from getting in touch with who we really are, when the temporary emotions and thoughts have passed. It's our true nature.

Imagine that your mind is a vast sky, a beautiful and peaceful blue. The sky goes on forever with no boundary or end in sight.

Take a moment to notice your thoughts as they pass through your awareness. Each passing thought is simply a cloud in your vast sky, temporary and fleeting.

Try to view each thought as a passing cloud. Let it fade in and out of your awareness, without pushing it away or grabbing on to it. Simply let it be and let it pass.

Throughout the day, many emotions and thoughts pass through you. Some are angry, some are joyful, and some are sad. Each one of these is just a temporary cloud in the sky of your awareness. The clouds pass, but the sky is always there.

This vast sky is your inner peace. It's the bright light that is always inside of you when the sky is calm. When it's cloudy, it can be hard to see it, but it's always there deep inside.

Rest with a sense of deep calm knowing that this inner peace is always there inside of you. You are safe. You are going to be okay.

Take a deep breath and feel into this deep sense of peace as much as you can. If thoughts, emotions, or physical sensations temporarily cloud this inner peace, that's okay. Just let them pass and continue to focus on the peaceful blue sky.

Think of a loved one you'd like to share this sense of peace with. It could be a partner, a family member, or a friend. Remember that this inner peace is vast and boundless like the sky. You can share this peace with others and still have an infinite amount for yourself.

Imagine your loved one in your mind and send these feelings of peace to them. "May you be at peace. May you be at peace."

Imagine sending this peace to the entire world. To all those who are in pain or suffering. To all those who want to be loved and happy. To all the humans, animals, and plants everywhere. "May you be at peace. May you be at peace."

Remember that this inner peace is as vast as the sky. You can share it openly with others and always have more for yourself. It is infinite. When you share this feeling of peace, you create a happier and safer world for yourself and others.

Take one more deep breath in, filling up with peace and love. Take a deep breath out, sending this peace and love out to the world. When you're ready, you can slowly bring your attention back into the room and open your eyes to end this meditation.

21

MEDITATION FOR CREATIVITY

Intention: Get in touch with your creative side.
Practices: Breath awareness, visualization.

Welcome to ***Day 21****! This meditation will help you release inhibitions, so you can unleash full self-expression and allow creativity to flow.*

While kids are encouraged to be creative, adults rarely are. As a result, our natural creativity often gets blocked and we end up feeling tired and unmotivated.

When creativity flows freely without inhibitions, we feel more motivated, energetic, and alive. Creativity means expressing yourself in your truest form without fear or holding back. This form of expression is a great release that will allow you to let go and relax more fully.

This meditation is especially beneficial for when you feel mentally blocked or stuck. It will help you to think outside the box and get those creative juices flowing!

Begin this meditation in a comfortable position. Find a position where you feel alert yet relaxed. Notice the natural curves of your spine as your body sinks into the earth.

Take a deep breath as you settle into the present moment. Notice where you feel the breath most strongly. Is it at the tip of the nose? The chest or maybe the belly? Wherever you feel the breath most strongly—bring your attention to rest there.

Notice how the breath naturally moves in and out of the body, all on its own. There is no need to force or control—the body has its own wisdom. Just relax into the breath and allow it to flow freely.

Imagine a brightly colored light streaming down from above you. This light is like a prism—you can see every color of the rainbow within it. There are shades of red, orange, yellow, green, blue, purple, and everything in between. Feel into the wonder of this beautiful rainbow light as you relax more deeply into your seat.

Imagine this rainbow light flowing into your head. As it swirls around, you can feel it stirring up the creativity deep inside of you.

This creativity has been locked away for a long time. Maybe due to embarrassment, lack of energy, or other inhibitions. Whatever the reason, it's in the past. Give the creativity inside of you permission to flow freely now, as this rainbow light continues to envelop you. When you let your inhibitions go, creativity can flow freely as inspiration flourishes.

Feel the creativity growing inside, as every thought and idea in your head is touched by this rainbow light. You feel more inspired and imaginative with every breath.

With nothing blocking your natural creativity, inspired ideas flow easily through your mind. You can do anything. You can be anything.

Imagine this rainbow light flowing into your heart now. True creativity comes from the heart, from the core of who you truly are. Let that creativity flow freely as the rainbow light fills your heart.

As creativity and imagination fill your heart, you feel inspired like you never have before. You realize that your imagination is boundless—you can be as creative as you want to be! There are no limits.

Notice your breath again. Feel how the breath continues to move in and out of the body, uninhibited. There are no blocks or obstacles—the breath simply flows. Allow your creativity to be like the breath, moving through your heart and mind freely without obstacles.

Imagine the rainbow light filling your whole body with creativity and vision. Rest in this warm and comforting glow as inspiration continues to flow.

Take one more deep breath, allowing the breath to flow freely inside of you. You are now filled with creativity, joy, and love. When you're ready, bring your attention back into the room and open your eyes to end this meditation.

22

MEDITATION FOR PATIENCE

Intention: Slow down the mind to cultivate patience.
Practices: Mindfulness, breath awareness, box breathing,
visualization, mantra.

Welcome to Day 22! Patience is an extremely valuable skill that grows with practice. This meditation is a reminder that everything happens in its time and in the right order. It will help you to slow down the mind and let things be, leading to a greater sense of peace and tranquility.

So often in life, we're jumping ahead and looking toward the future. While the future can be exciting, it hasn't happened yet. Meditation brings us into the present moment and allows us to rest our busy minds, even briefly.

This meditation involves a technique called box breathing. With box breathing, you breathe in through the nose, hold the breath, breathe out through the mouth, and then hold the breath again. Each of these four basic steps, lasts for 4 seconds.

Remember that everything in life happens in its own time. This doesn't mean that we stop trying to achieve our goals. It simply means we don't *need to achieve them all <u>right now,</u> in order to be happy. Happiness does not depend on achieving a goal in the future. You can be happy in the here and now too.*

The mantra for this meditation is "Be present. Be patient. Be calm."

Find a comfortable position either sitting up or lying down. Gently close your eyes and allow yourself to let go and just rest.

Start by noticing your breath. Is the breath quick and shallow? Or is it slow and deep? Just notice without altering the breath in any way.

The breath and the mind are connected. When the breath is quick, the mind tends to run quickly as well. When we slow down the breath, we create more space in the mind. This is the start of cultivating patience.

Box breathing is a simple way to calm the nervous system and cultivate patience. It clears the mind of distractions and releases tension.

You'll start by inhaling for a count of four, holding the breath for a count of four, exhaling for a count of four, then holding the breath for a count of four. The consistency of this breath is very soothing to both the mind and the body.

Practice three rounds of box breathing and then take a natural inhale and exhale. Observe the mind after a few rounds of box breathing. Has the mind slowed down? If not, that's okay. Just notice.

This slow consistent breathing calms the mind and cultivates patience. Briefly holding the breath creates a bit of space for the mind and body to just rest.

Next, bring to mind the image of a pink flower bud. Everything in nature blooms in its own time. With patience, this small bud will blossom into a beautiful flower.

Take one last slow, deep breath, holding it at the top, and exhaling completely. Fully experience the beauty of this moment and allow things to be exactly as they are right now.

Be present. Be patient. Be calm.

Whenever you feel the mind jumping ahead, worried about the future, simply slow down the breath to slow down the mind. Remember that everything happens in its own time and allow yourself to let go and just trust.

Be present. Be patient. Be calm.

Take one last deep breath and when you're ready, slowly bring your attention back into the room and gently open your eyes to end this meditation.

23

MEDITATION FOR DIGITAL DETOX

<u>Intention:</u> Reset your mind and body from the constant exposure to screens and technology.
<u>Practices:</u> Mindfulness, breath awareness, body awareness.

*Welcome to **Day 23**! This meditation is a short "digital detox" that will give you a complete rest from screens and electronic devices.*

A digital detox is simply a period of time where you refrain from using electronic devices. This could be just a few minutes or several days.

This meditation will give you a complete reset in just minutes! In a world where we're constantly on our screens, it's become more important than ever to take the time to unplug and just rest. With this practice, you will take a rest from screens, electronic devices, and social media. You will rest your eyes and take a much-needed break from technology.

It can be difficult to detach from our screens because they make us feel productive and connected. However, taking short technology breaks throughout the day (1–2 minutes with your eyes closed) can actually help you get more done.

If you'd like to take this practice even further, you could set an intention to limit screens for the day. This is totally optional, but can help you detox from screens more completely.

Begin this meditation by finding a comfortable position either sitting up or lying down. Relax the muscles around your eyes and allow them to close. Bring your attention to the breath.

Take a deep breath and allow your mind to clear. All the thoughts and emotions from your busy day—just let them all go. You don't need them for this practice. Give yourself permission to relax and be present.

Allow your body to relax and unwind as you sink deeper into your seat. Notice where there are any areas of tension in the body and just allow them to release.

Notice the muscles in your forehead and around your eyes. These areas get very strained from use throughout the day, so give them permission to relax completely. You don't need to use your eyes right now—let them soften and release.

As you continue breathing in and out, notice how your body gently shifts from "doing" mode into "being" mode. Most of the time, we're in "doing" mode. We're working, answering emails, or scrolling through social media, and we do most of this on autopilot without even thinking about it. When we shift into "being" mode, we allow ourselves to simply be in the moment. There's nothing to do right now and no place to go except to just be here, observing the breath and relaxing the mind.

If your mind wanders away from the present moment into what you need to do later today, simply notice and bring your attention back to the breath and the body. When we shift our attention into the physical body, our mind relaxes.

We spend so much of the day in our own heads—worrying about this or thinking about that. This is your time to relax into your body and just be.

As you prepare to resume your day, remember that you can always take a pause when you need it. A few times a day, make a conscious decision to step away from your screens, close your eyes, and just be. Give yourself permission to take a break, even for just a few seconds. It will help you to continue your day from a place of calm and ease.

Take one more deep breath in, filling the body and the lungs completely, and breathe out, letting everything go. When you're ready, you can slowly bring your attention back into the room and open your eyes to end this meditation.

24

MEDITATION TO CALM THE MIND

<u>Intention:</u> Let go of thoughts, so you can relax the mind fully.
<u>Practices:</u> Mindfulness, breath awareness.

*Welcome to **Day 24**! Your intention for this practice is simple: relax the mind by focusing on the breath. This is a simple, but very effective mindfulness practice.*

When you focus on the breath, the mind becomes clear and calm. If your mind wanders away from the breath during this meditation, that's perfectly fine. Simply bring your attention back to the breath as you continue to calm the mind.

You can do this meditation to quiet the mind before bed or any time during the day when you're feeling overwhelmed by thoughts. This meditation is a quick and effective way to bring yourself back to center any time you need it.

Begin this meditation in a comfortable position either sitting up or lying down. Gently close your eyes and bring your attention to the breath.

Take a few deep, slow breaths in through the nose and out through the mouth. Allow your body to settle and relax into the furniture.

Notice where you feel the breath the most strongly. This could be at the tip of the nose, the chest, or the belly. Wherever you feel the breath the most strongly, bring your attention to rest there.

During this meditation, you will be focusing your attention on the breath to calm the mind. If you find your attention wandering away from the breath into thinking, that is completely fine and expected. Simply acknowledge where your attention has gone and gently guide it back to the breath.

For the duration of this meditation, focus your attention on the breath to quiet your mind. Allow the thoughts to pass through your awareness, as you bring your attention back to the breath, each time it wanders. This practice doesn't require any thinking. Simply give your mind permission to relax and let go.

As you prepare to reengage with your day, remember that when your mind is super busy or overwhelmed, you can always take a moment to tune into your breath to quiet the mind.

Take one more slow, deep breath, in through the nose, and out through the mouth, allowing any remaining thoughts to pass through your awareness. When you're ready, you can slowly bring your attention back into the room and open your eyes to end this meditation.

25

MEDITATION FOR KINDNESS

Intention: Open your heart and show genuine kindness toward
yourself and others.
Practices: Visualization, compassion, positive memory recall,
mantra.

*Welcome to **Day 25**! This meditation is a reminder of how important it is to be kind to one another.*

You'll start by thinking of a time when someone was kind to you and then you'll capture that feeling in your heart. At the end of the meditation, you'll think of one kind thing you can do for someone else.

Inside each one of us is a kind and warm heart. We simply need to take the time to connect with that kindness and share it with the world. You will feel a radiant sense of warmth and kindness during and after this meditation that will fill your heart with happiness.

The mantra for this meditation is "Be calm. Be happy. Be kind."

Kindness is contagious! Pay it forward.

Begin this meditation in a comfortable position either sitting up or lying down. Gently close your eyes and bring your attention to the breath.

Take a deep breath in, filling up with kindness and love. Breathe out, letting the warmth of kindness wash over you. Bring a slight smile to your lips as you continue to breathe deeply.

Start by bringing to mind a time when someone was kind to you. Think about how this act of kindness made you feel. Does it bring a smile to your face when you think about it? Do you feel a sense of warmth inside of you? Take a moment to really get in touch with how this act of kindness made you feel.

Imagine that the feelings of warmth and happiness from this act of kindness are flowing through you like liquid gold, warming you up from head to toe.

Feel the warmth of kindness in your feet, flowing up through your legs, your hips, your stomach, and your chest.

Feel the warmth flow through your heart, as you relax a little more deeply into your seat. Visualize this liquid gold kindness filling your heart, making you feel happy and warm.

Feel the warmth flow up through your shoulders and down your arms, then into your hands. Feel it radiate up through your neck and into your head.

Let warm and genuine kindness fill up your heart and body as you continue to rest peacefully.

Be calm. Be happy. Be kind.

Be calm. Be happy. Be kind.

As you bring this meditation to a close, think about one kind thing you can do for someone else today. This can be just a small thing like holding the door or giving someone a genuine compliment. An act of kindness, no matter how small, radiates outward bringing happiness to others, as well as yourself.

Take one more deep breath, allowing that liquid gold to fill you up even more with a kindness that radiates out to the whole world.

Be calm. Be happy. Be kind.

When you're ready, you can slowly bring your attention back into the room and gently open your eyes to end this meditation.

26

MEDITATION FOR OPEN AWARENESS

Intention: Broaden your perspective by experimenting with various anchors for your attention.
Practices: Mindfulness, open (or choiceless) awareness.

*Welcome to **Day 26**! This meditation will help you to develop a broad and balanced perspective. With open awareness (sometimes called choiceless awareness), we allow all the different aspects of our awareness to coexist in harmony.*

In meditation, an "anchor" is simply what you choose to focus your attention on in the moment. With this practice, you will be shifting your focus between several different anchors. You'll start by focusing on one anchor at a time and then, at the end, you'll open up and allow all of them to simply pass through your awareness.

The structure of this practice will be as follows:

1. *Awareness of the breath*
2. *Awareness of sounds*
3. *Awareness of physical sensations*

4. *Awareness of thoughts*
5. *Awareness of emotions*
6. *Open awareness*

As you move your awareness between these different anchors, simply observe without judgment, being careful not to label what comes up as "good" or "bad." There's no need to judge or control—you are simply the observer.

Through this practice, you will grow to understand the fleeting nature of emotions, sensations, and thoughts, so you can maintain a balanced sense of perspective.

Find a comfortable position either sitting up or lying down. Gently close your eyes and bring your attention to the breath.

The meditation practice of open or choiceless awareness is a unique and very effective one. It teaches the brain to hold more than one anchor in its awareness creating a more balanced perspective.

This practice is particularly useful when dealing with difficult emotions, such as anger or anxiety. When we're experiencing strong emotion, we tend to focus our attention on it, which makes it difficult to let it go. We continue to feed the emotion with our thoughts causing the feeling to take over and overwhelm us. Practicing open awareness helps us to shift attention during these difficult moments, creating more space to breathe and return to calm.

Start by focusing your attention on the breath. Feel into where you feel the breath most strongly and bring your attention to rest there. If the mind wanders away from the breath, that's completely fine. Just gently bring your attention back and continue to observe the breath.

Shift your attention to sounds. What do you hear? Allow the sounds around you to rise and fall in your awareness. Focus on each sound as it arises and then disappears. Just like when you were focusing on the breath, if your mind wanders, that's okay. Just bring your attention back to focusing on sounds.

Gently shift your awareness to physical sensations. Bring your attention to the body and just notice what comes up. There might be tingling, numbness, or a sense of warmth. Simply allow these sensations to be there, as they rise and fall in your awareness. Try not to label these sensations as "good" or "bad"—simply observe them. If your mind wanders, just bring it back to the physical sensations in the body.

Shift your attention to your thoughts. Notice each thought as it arises in your mind without pushing it away or clinging to it. Simply let each thought arise and then disappear making room for the next thought.

If you notice yourself getting lost in a particular thought, bring your attention back to simply observing each thought in a neutral way. The difference between observing thoughts and getting lost in them is subtle, but important. See if you can notice the difference during your practice.

Shift your attention to emotions. Notice any emotions that are rising and falling inside of you. What thoughts and physical sensations are associated with this emotion? Try not to feed or get lost in the emotion. Simply observe it in your body.

Now open up your awareness, letting go of any particular object of attention. Simply notice anything that comes into your awareness —this may be the breath, sounds, physical sensations, thoughts, or emotions. Don't focus on any one of them in particular; simply let them come in and out of your awareness on their own.

This practice can be challenging at first, so if you need to, you can always bring your attention back to the breath and then resume the open awareness practice when you're ready.

When we get angry, anxious, or stressed, it's often because we're focusing on just one aspect of our awareness. We're focusing all our attention on a thought, emotion, or a narrative in our head. During these moments, it's helpful to broaden our perspective and notice other aspects of our awareness: the breath, sounds, physical sensations, and so on. As you do this, you'll notice that the stressful emotions start to lose their power over you. When you broaden your perspective, you create more space for balance and equanimity.

Take one more deep breath, in through the nose, and out through the mouth. When you're ready, you can slowly bring your attention back into the room and open your eyes to end this meditation.

27

MEDITATION FOR LETTING GO

<u>Intention:</u> Let go of chasing your thoughts, so you can enter a state of just being.
<u>Practices</u>: Mindfulness, visualization, breath awareness, mantra.

*Welcome to **Day 27**! This meditation will help you relax and let go by teaching you to observe your thoughts without getting lost in them. It involves seeing your thoughts as just "mental events" and watching them as an impartial observer.*

Letting go is one of the most difficult, but important skills to master. It requires letting go of the story in your head of how things <u>should</u> be, and simply accepting them as they <u>are</u>. This means allowing thoughts to pass through the mind without grasping on to them.

This meditation will help you to release and let go, so you can feel calm and peaceful at a very deep level.

The mantra for this meditation is "Let go." You can think to yourself "let" on the in-breath and "go" on the out-breath.

Begin this meditation in a comfortable position either sitting up or lying down. Take a deep breath in through your nose and out through your mouth. Allow your body to settle deeply into the earth.

The practice of letting go will help you approach life with more calm and awareness. It begins with letting go of any thoughts or emotions that are looping in your mind from the day. Any stress or anxiety that you feel from earlier in the day, simply let it go. You don't need it for this practice. This is your time to relax and let go.

Imagine that you are sitting on the edge of a river. You can hear the birds chirping and the sounds of nature all around you. As you sit, the water gently flows by.

As you look closer, you notice leaves floating by on the surface of the water. You observe the closest leaf until it floats further down the river and out of sight. Then, you turn your attention to the next leaf and the one after that, as each leaf slowly passes in and then out of your awareness.

Each leaf is like a thought passing through the mind. If you don't try to touch it or grab on to it, it simply floats by all on its own.

Try to observe each of your thoughts as a passing leaf floating through your awareness. Simply let it be there and then let it go, without getting lost in the story of the thought. It is simply another leaf on the river—let it come and let it pass.

Bring your attention to the breath. Take a deep breath in and think to yourself "let." Then, breathe out and think to yourself "go." Breathe in "let" and breathe out "go."

Focus your full attention on the breath paired with the mantra "let go." The words will help steady your attention and remind the brain that it's time to "let go" of thoughts and just be present.

Take one more full deep breath and breathe out, letting it all go. When you're ready, you can slowly bring your attention back into the room and open your eyes to end this meditation.

28

MEDITATION FOR EMBRACING CHANGE

<u>Intention:</u> Learn to accept and even embrace change as a natural part of life.
<u>Practices:</u> Mindfulness, breath awareness, visualization, mantra.

*Welcome to **Day 28**! The only constant in life is change. This idea can feel a bit scary at first, but once you embrace it, you'll truly be living life to the fullest!*

As humans, we tend to resist change, even positive change. This is due to our inherent fear of the unknown. We generally prefer to stay in our bubble where it's comfortable and "safe." But, no matter how much you try to avoid it, change always comes. Nothing stays the same in life.

Everything is constantly flowing and changing: our thoughts, our bodies, and all that is around us. Learning to embrace change, instead of resisting it, puts us into the flow of life. This results in less stress and more positive energy.

The mantra for this meditation is "I accept and embrace change."

Begin this meditation in a comfortable position either sitting up or lying down. Take a deep breath and gently close your eyes.

Bring your attention to the breath. Notice the gentle rise and fall of the inhale and exhale. Try not to alter or control the breath in any way. Just breathe naturally and gently, allowing the breath to flow freely through you.

The concept of change can be a source of stress or anxiety for many of us—the fear of the unknown. The key to inviting positive change into our lives is learning to embrace the uncertainty, instead of resisting or fearing it. Change is a natural and unavoidable part of life, so we teach our brains to accept and even welcome what is already inevitable.

Breathe naturally and notice how the breath changes from one moment to the next. No two breaths are exactly the same. Sometimes the breath is quick and shallow, and other times, it's slow and deep. Your breath is always changing. Your body is always changing. Your mind is always changing.

Take a moment to observe the changes that are going on inside and around you right now. Observe how thoughts, sensations, and sounds are constantly changing.

Now imagine that you're sitting or lying down outside in nature. You could be in a park, a garden, or a meadow. Whatever feels right to you. The sun is shining, the birds are chirping, and the sky feels vast and open. You relax a little more deeply into the earth as you take in this beautiful and open space.

You look up at the blue sky above you and see clouds floating by. Notice the shapes of the clouds and observe how they change as they move across the sky. The clouds are always changing and shifting. They never stay constant or still. Continue to observe the changing clouds as you rest in your beautiful place. Allow each cloud to change and pass without clinging on to it.

Relax more deeply knowing that everything changes. Change is the one constant in life. The more you learn to embrace change, the more you'll be able to relax and let go.

Repeat this mantra to yourself: I accept and embrace change. I accept and embrace change. I accept and embrace change.

As you bring this meditation to a close, take a few moments to invite positive change into your life. Don't resist it and don't fear it. Simply welcome it with open arms and a smile in your heart. You can accept change and you can embrace it. Change is growth. Change is life.

When you're ready, you can slowly bring your attention back into the room and open your eyes to end this meditation.

29

MEDITATION FOR PAIN RELIEF

Intention: Relax the body by observing physical sensations with compassionate acceptance.
Practices: Mindfulness, breath awareness, body awareness, compassionate acceptance.

*Welcome to **Day 29**! This meditation relaxes the body, which can help to reduce physical pain. This practice is similar to impartially observing thoughts in the Meditation for Letting Go on Day 27, but you'll be observing physical sensations instead.*

While this meditation relieves pain very effectively, you don't have to be in pain right now to benefit from it. Observing physical sensations is simply another anchor for your attention.

This meditation will help you relax by moving your attention away from thoughts and into the physical body. While observing the body may seem counterintuitive when it comes to pain, it's exactly what we need to feel better. What we resist, persists, so if we open up and learn to accept our pain, even a little bit, it diminishes.

The core of this practice is observing physical sensations with acceptance and compassion.

Note: For tomorrow's meditation (Day 30), you will need a small piece of food, such as a slice of apple, a chocolate square, or a raisin. Make sure it's small enough that it can be eaten in just a few bites.

Begin this meditation in a comfortable position either sitting up or lying down. Take a few moments to position your body with care and compassion. You can even stretch and loosen up your muscles a bit. If it feels good to you, you can move your head gently from side to side to release your neck. Find a position where you feel alert yet relaxed.

Take a deep breath in, filling up your whole body with the loving and compassionate breath. Breathe out allowing your body to relax and release.

If you find yourself in any pain during this meditation, that's okay. Just continue to breathe through it, as you allow your body to sink more deeply into gravity. Feel how gravity supports your body as you rest.

Bring your attention to the physical sensations in the body. Notice how the body feels today. You may feel tingling, warmth, itching, or any other array of sensations. If you take the time to pay attention to the body, you'll notice sensations that are constantly shifting.

Observe the changing sensations in your body. If your mind wanders into thoughts, gently bring it back to the physical body.

When we're in any kind of pain, whether it be emotional or physical, our instinct is to push it away. Unfortunately, that only makes the sensations stronger. What we resist, persists, so just take a moment to invite the sensations into your awareness and just observe.

This kind of compassionate acceptance of our pain is difficult to master, but it is a science-based way to effectively reduce pain. It's been said that pain is inevitable, but suffering is optional. Continue to observe the physical sensations in your body with compassion and acceptance.

If you are in pain today, see if you can notice any pleasant sensations in the body. When the body is hurting, we tend to focus our attention on the sensations of pain. But, if you really take the time to notice, you'll begin to observe other sensations as well, maybe even pleasant ones like warmth in your hands or a softness in your face.

Take a few moments to notice pleasant sensations in the body. When we can accept our pain and shift our attention away from it, it begins to fade into the background.

By focusing attention on physical sensations, you are also bringing yourself into the present moment, the here and now. When your mind starts wandering off, worrying about this or that, simply bring your attention to the physical sensations in the body. This will center you in the present moment.

When you're able to let go of the thoughts associated with physical pain and just focus on the sensations themselves, pain diminishes. This takes time and practice, but eventually, pain diminishes. All pain whether physical or emotional is just temporary. Let it be there and then let it pass.

Take one more deep breath filling the body, once more, with compassion and love. When you're ready, you can slowly bring your attention back into the room and open your eyes to end this meditation.

30

MINDFUL EATING MEDITATION

Intention: To savor one small piece of food with intention and mindfulness.
Practice: Mindful eating.

*Welcome to **Day 30**! This meditation will teach you to enjoy a small piece of food mindfully. When you learn to slow down and savor your food, you automatically consume only the amount that your body needs to feel satisfied.*

You will need a small piece of a food for this meditation, such as a slice of apple, a chocolate square, or a raisin. Make sure it's small enough that it can be eaten in just a few bites.

Mindful eating is the process of understanding your thought patterns, emotional moods, and habits when it comes to food. It involves paying full attention to the experience of eating—just like you would with the breath in mindfulness meditation.

Mindful eating is a science-based way to lose weight and keep it off permanently. It helps your digestive system by encouraging you to slow down and savor your food. You can practice mindful eating daily to build healthier eating habits.

*If you're interested in losing weight with meditation, be sure to check out my other book, **Meditation for Weight Loss**. This is a complete program that includes audio recordings, worksheets, checklists, a 30-day plan, and all the other tools you'll need to successfully lose weight <u>without</u> dieting or working out!*

Begin this meditation in a comfortable position sitting up. Sit up tall through the spine and allow the breath to flow freely through you, filling you with energy and positivity.

Take a deep and mindful breath, paying full attention to the sensation of breathing as you breathe in and out. Bring your full attention to the breath as it continues to move in and out of the body all on its own. If your mind wanders, gently bring it back and continue to observe the breath mindfully.

Mindful eating is the practice of paying full attention to the experience of eating. It works similarly to paying full attention to the breath —it's simply a different anchor. You'll focus your awareness on the sensations of eating and bring your mind back when it wanders.

Bring your attention to the piece of food in front of you. Place the food in your hand and notice how it looks and feels. What color is it? How big is it? How does it feel against your skin? Simply observe the food with full and open awareness. If your mind wanders, bring it back to focusing on the food in your hand.

Take a small bite of the food and hold it in your mouth for a few seconds. Notice the texture and taste. What flavors do you taste? How does it feel in your mouth?

Slowly chew and swallow the food. Be aware of the sensations. What can you hear, taste, and feel?

Continue to eat the food mindfully taking small bites and feeling into the taste, texture, and sensations of eating. If your mind wanders, bring it back to the experience of eating.

Make a commitment to yourself to eat at least one piece of food mindfully each day. Learn to savor and enjoy your food—this is an act of self-care.

Before you sit down to eat your next meal, take a slight pause and ask your body which foods would be most nourishing for you today. Enjoy your food without distraction—turn off the TV and your smartphone. Be aware of how you eat and consciously slow down, if you're eating too fast. Give the experience of eating your full attention and be on the lookout for fullness cues. When you feel satisfied, stop eating and take a deep breath.

Mindful eating is a practice. It takes time and patience, but it's extremely effective for those looking to lose weight or eat healthier.

Take one more deep breath, filling your body up with self-love and self-care. When you're ready, you can slowly bring your attention back into the room to end this meditation.

CLOSING NOTES

Congratulations—you did it! You've completed a daily meditation each day for 30 days. You've built a healthy habit that will help you live every day with confidence and calm.

In order to maintain your practice, commit to continuing with the daily meditations, as much as possible. Feel free to choose your practice based on what feels right to you on that particular day. For example, if you're experiencing brain fog, you could practice the Meditation for Focus from Day 4.

These meditations are here for you any time you need them! They are uniquely designed to address a variety of everyday issues, concerns, and stressors, so there's always something you can tap into in order to manage your day. Consider this book to be your own personal meditation toolbox!

Meditation is a healthy and science-based habit that you can turn to any time. Be sure to continue practicing the skills and intentions that resonate with you. You can also feel free to repeat the 30 days any time you need it!

If you enjoyed this book and are interested in utilizing meditation to lose weight, eliminate unhealthy cravings, and create a positive body image, be sure to check out *Meditation for Weight Loss*.

I would also appreciate it so much, if you could leave a rating or review for this book on Amazon! Your feedback means the world to me and helps me bring more books to you.

BONUS: MEDITATION JOURNAL

In order to delve more deeply into your daily practice, you can reflect on your experiences through journaling. This is totally optional, but can help you connect more deeply with the themes and intentions of your practice.

If you would like a printable PDF meditation journal to accompany your practice, you can sign up at boundlessbooks.kit.com/journal and we'll send it straight to your inbox!

REFERENCES

Meditation 101 by Inner IDEA

What Is the Best Type of Meditation? by Peter Morales-Brown

7 Scientifically Proven Benefits of Gratitude by Amy Morin

How Meditation Benefits Your Mind and Body by Matthew Thorpe, MD, PhD

ABOUT THE AUTHOR

Alyssa Reynolds is a health coach and the founder of Flaxseeds & Fairytales. She teaches a practical approach to meditation that reduces stress and promotes well-being in just minutes a day. Her goal is to help clients and readers achieve radiant health from the inside out. In her free time, Alyssa enjoys ballroom dancing, cozy mysteries, and developing healthy recipes.

Made in United States
Orlando, FL
10 June 2025

62017820R00069